A PROFORÇA TH
IN ASSOCATION WI

FLASHBANG

BY JAMES LEWIS

Published by Playdead Press 2024

© James Lewis 2024

James Lewis has asserted his rights under the Copyright, Design and Patents Act, 1988, to be identified as the author of this work.

A CIP catalogue record for this book is available from the British Library.

ISBN 978-1-915533-22-7

Caution

All rights whatsoever in this play are strictly reserved and application for performance should be sought through Proforça Theatre Company before rehearsals begin. No performance may be given unless a license has been obtained. Please contact via Proforça Theatre Company, C/O Theataccounts, 1 The Oakley, Kidderminster Road, Droitwich, Worcs, WR9 0AY. Or by email to hello@proforca.co.uk with the subject - FLASHBANG - PERFORMANCE RIGHTS.

This book is sold subject to the condition that it shall not by way of trade or otherwise, be lent, resold, hired out, or otherwise circulated without the publisher's prior consent in any form of binding or cover other than that in which it is published and without a similar condition including this condition being imposed on the subsequent purchaser.

Playdead Press
www.playdeadpress.com

CAST & CREATIVES [2024]

Ryan / Ryan   Nick Hardie
Ryan / Jason   Benjamin Booth-Bennett
Ryan / Andy   Matt Wake
Ryan / Deano   Fred Wardale

With Dan Nash as **Mikey** & Lauren Ferdinand as **Shanice.**

Flashbang was originally performed in September 2022 at the Lion & Unicorn Theatre, Kentish Town, Produced by **Proforça Theatre Company.** The original cast were:

Ryan / Ryan   Sam Kacher
Ryan / Jason   Emmanuel Olusanya
Ryan / Andy   Henry Brackenridge
Ryan / Deano   Fred Wardale

With Dan Nash as **Mikey** & Lauren Ferdinand as **Shanice.**

For Proforça Theatre Company:
Written by: James Lewis
Directed by: David Brady
Movement Director: Lucy Glassbrook
Associate Director: Jess Barton
Lighting / Sound Design: Proforca Theatre Company
Public Relations: Matthew Parker
Additional Marketing: Terri Paddock – MyTheatreMates
Legal Services: Alletsons Solicitors
Accountancy Services: Theataccounts (theataccounts.co.uk)
Consulting Producer: Antony Stuart-Hicks
Production Photography & Cover Image: Ross Kernahan
Original Casting by: Suzy Catliff

For the Lion & Unicorn Theatre:
Artistic Director: David Brady
FOH Duty Managers: Nance Turner, Jakey Newton, Emma Burnell & Grace Gjertsen.

The Producers Wish To Thank:

Marian & John Brady, Anthony Fagan, Ben Borthwick, Vicki Marsh, Vicki Macgregor, Hannah Daniels, Avi & the team at the Lion & Unicorn Pub, Catrin Bailey-Jones & Paris Bailey-Jones, Harriet Lambert, Erin Read, Melissa Phillips, Olivia Thompson, Kim Scopes, Everything Theatre, Heather Jeffrey & London Pub Theatres, Kieran Doherty, The Associate Artists of the Lion & Unicorn Theatre 2019-2023. Georgie Bailey, Hal Darling & Lucy Betts, Mark Conway, David Meredith, Kevin Shaw & the Albany Theatre Coventry, James Edge & the Old Joint Stock Theatre Birmingham, Alex Dyer, Young's Pubs & everyone who else who has supported *Flashbang* on its journey.

CAST

Nick Hardie | Ryan / Ryan

Nick's previous work includes: *Romeo & Juliet* (East London Shakespeare Festival, Dir. Rosie Ward); *Gloria* (Mountview Academy, Dir. Matthew Dunster); *Witness for the Prosecution* (The County Hall London, Dir. Lucy Bailey); *Doctors* (BBC Studios, Dir. Ita Fitzgerald); *Carte D'Or Commercial* (DDB UK LTD, Dir. Andrew Chaplin); *Magic at the Musicals* (Magic FM, Dir. Jon Ranger).

Previous work for Proforça includes: The Shatterbox (Dir. David Brady)

Nick is an Associate Artist of Proforça Theatre Company.

Benjamin Booth-Bennett | Ryan / Jason

Benjamin is an actor based in London currently training at The London Meisner Company. He began his training at Sylvia Young Theatre school and has since worked on various film projects, including the multi-award winning *The Immunda Experiment* and *The Last Day* for Sky Arts.

He has also trained in various styles of dance and is skilled behind the camera, having worked on numerous media projects and leisurely pursuing photography.

Flashbang is Benjamin's professional London stage debut.

Matt Wake | Ryan / Andy

Matt grew up in Hertfordshire and graduated from Guildford School of Acting in 2021.

His theatre credits include originating the role of "Callum" in *Lately* and "Captain Phillips" in *48* (Proforça Theatre Company); *The Players of Dieudone* (Hideout Theatre) and

The Last Laugh (Take Note Theatre). Most recently, Matt played Romeo in the Young Shakespeare Company's tour of *Romeo & Juliet*. In 2023, Matt worked on his first feature film, *Melodrive* (M&M Film Productions), which is to be released later this year.

Matt is a founding member and associate artist of Hideout Theatre and is currently developing Hideout's next production.

Matt is an Associate Artist of Proforca Theatre Company.

Fred Wardale | Callum / Cal

Fred is an actor from the East Midlands who graduated from Royal Birmingham Conservatoire. Previous work with the company includes originating the role of Deano in the critically-acclaimed first run production of *Flashbang* [2023] and originating the role of Callum (alongside Matt Wake) in the original, Offie-nominated run of *Lately* (Lion & Unicorn Theatre & UK Tour, 2021/23).

Fred has worked on various short films and voiceover projects. He is also a writer, regularly creating his own material, with his first play currently in the works.

Fred is an Associate Artist of Proforca Theatre Company.

Dan Nash | Mikey

Dan trained in acting at Italia Conti, graduating in 2020. He's a Brummie lad based in London.

His recent credits include the 2024 tour of *Jekyll & Hyde* for the National Theatre; *All's Well That Ends Well* (UK Tour); *48, AAAAA* (Proforça Theatre Company) and *The Sonnet Project* (Jermyn Street Theatre).

Credits whilst training include *The Accrington Pals*, *Love and Information* and *Almost, Maine* (Lion & Unicorn Theatre and Edinburgh Fringe).

Lauren Ferdinand | Alison / Alf

Lauren trained at Rose Bruford & The National Youth Theatre. Previous work includes originating the role of Alf in *Lately* (Proforça Theatre Company, Lion & Unicorn Theatre, Albany Theatre, UK Tour, 2021/23); *Volcano*, Flashbang (also Proforça Theatre Company); *Before Feel* (Lion & Unicorn Theatre) and *Best Served Cold* (Leicester Curve).

Credit whilst training include *White Millionaire Emmas*; *Ghosts* and *Cleansed*

Lauren is an Associate Artist of Proforça Theatre Company.

CREATIVES

James Lewis | Writer

James Lewis is a critically-acclaimed & award nominated writer based in London. Previous credits include *If I Go* (2016); *Feel* (2018/19,UK Tour); *Reading Gaol* (2017/18); *At Last* (2019); *AAAAA [FiveA]* (2021); *Lately* (2021, UK Tour); *Volcano* (2022); *Flashbang* (2022) and *The Shatter Box* (2023).

James also contributed the pieces *Charlie* (2018), *Georgie* (2019), *Ryan* (2020) and *Euan* (2023) to Proforca's *Feel More* anthology companion to *Feel*, plus the short piece *By Your Side* which is currently in development as a short film.

At Last, AAAAA, Lately & *The Shatter Box* were all nominated for Standing Ovation Awards by London Pub Theatres Magazine and *Lately* was nominated for an Offie in 2021 for Best New Play.

Both *Lately* & *Flashbang* are published by Playdead Press.

David Brady | Director

David is an Offie-Nominated Writer, Director, and Artistic Director from Coventry based in London.

For Proforça credits include: *If I Go* (2016); *Saucy Jack & The Space Vixens* (2016); *The Importance of Being Earnest* (2017); *Reading Gaol* (2017-18); *Feel* (2018-19); *Feel More* (2018-2020); *At Last* (2019); *AAAAA [FiveA]* (2021); the Offie Nominated *Lately* (2021 & UK Tour 2022); *Flashbang* (2022/2024) and *The Shatter Box* (2023).

Other credits include *Getting Rid* (2018) for Actor Awareness; work for Far Cry Theatre (2019) and Associate

Producer of *BLUEBIRD* (2018) and *2nd Coming Again* (2018 - 2019).

He has directed work at YORAC, Theatre N16, The King's Head Theatre, Hertford Theatre, Upstairs at the Western, The Space & The Albany Theatre Coventry (amongst others). David is also the Artistic Director of the Lion & Unicorn Theatre in Kentish Town and was awarded a special commendation for services to Pub Theatre in 2021 by London Pub Theatres Magazine.

Lucy Glassbrook | Movement & Intimacy Director

Lucy is a Movement Director and choreographer, working with small casts on stories with brilliant storytelling. As a creator she is inspired by encounters with people from all walks of life, drawing inspiration from the communities the stories live within. She works with intimacy guidelines and her creation process journeys through embodied understanding and creating a culture of respect.

Her recent work includes: *Lately*, *Volcano*, *Flashbang* (Proforça Theatre Company); *Coventry City of Culture Opening Ceremony*; *Fighting Irish* (The Belgrade Theatre) and the Opening & Closing Ceremonies for the Commonwealth Games.

PROFORÇA THEATRE COMPANY

Proforça Theatre Company is an award-nominated, critically-acclaimed theatre company based in London.

It is our mission to create great theatre experiences which challenge, entertain, and confront our audiences.

Proforça Theatre Company was founded in late 2015. In addition to running a theatre company designed to promote and support the work of writers, actors, and directors through the creation of brilliant new fringe theatre work. We're also the managing company in charge of running and programming The Lion & Unicorn Theatre in Kentish Town.

Since 2016 we've presented new pieces of writing such as *If I Go* and the critically acclaimed and very successful expanded universes of *Feel* and *Feel More*; *Volcano* & *Flashbang* as well as new takes on exiting work such as *The Importance of Being Earnest*; a compelling fusion of original text and new writing in a remix of *Reading Gaol* and the musical *Saucy Jack & The Space Vixens*.

We have a reputation for high quality, high integrity fringe theatre which champions and showcases the talents of emerging creatives of all kinds.

We work hard to make sure that we operate with high standards of integrity and stewardship, and ensure that we take the utmost care of everyone we work with. We are commercially savvy and exceptionally well organised, and are starting to build some great relationships with venues and other companies outside of the London area, which we hope to continue to build as we embark on future projects. We believe this gives us an advantage and something unique we can offer over other theatre companies in the capital.

We try to create a "Proforça" way of doing things, not only within the company, but in making partnerships and supporting other performers, companies and artists. We're part of a fantastic network of London theatre-makers, and we love being a part of such an amazingly creative group of companies, talented individuals, and fully embrace the role we play in the fringe theatre community.

Website: www.proforca.co.uk

Social Media: @proforcatheatre

LION & UNICORN THEATRE

The Lion & Unicorn Theatre is a 60-seat black box studio theatre based above the Lion & Unicorn pub at the heart of Kentish Town, with Camden Town just a stone's throw away.

The venue is led by Artistic Director **David Brady** and provides a great home for the best in fringe theatre talent that London has to offer and we are keen to provide a warm, nurturing, and brilliant experience for both theatre makers and audiences alike.

In addition, the theatre supports new writing, and provides opportunities for a team of Associate Artists which includes a brilliant cross section of London fringe theatre creatives.

Since **Proforça Theatre Company** assumed responsibility for operating the venue in March 2019 we have not only developed a reputation for programming new and exciting work from some of the best theatre makers in London, we've made the venue both profitable as well as re-establishing the theatre as a destination fringe theatre venue with most productions in our inaugural seasons winning critical acclaim and award nominations.

The Lion & Unicorn Pub offers a brilliant pre and post show experience, with premium beers, wines and spirits as well as a fantastic and varied food menu offering great pub food. For a night of culture and excellent hospitality, there is no better place to spend an evening than at one of London's most well-respected pub theatres.

We are always looking to develop and enhance our creative partnerships, and we welcome any discussions about future reciprocal touring arrangements which may enhance our ability to support producers who may be interested in supporting the theatre for other projects. We have a vibrant and viable asset which other theatre companies are not necessarily able to offer prospective producing partners and are keen to promote these opportunities in 2024 and beyond.

Website: www.thelionandunicorntheatre.com

Social Media: @landutheatre

Flashbang is dedicated to Mark, and all the boys that come from brilliant towns 20 miles away from anywhere important...

CHARACTERS

MAIN CHARACTERS:

Ryan / Ryan: Early 20's, M,

Ryan / Jason: Early 20's, M

Ryan / Andy: Early 20's, M

Ryan / Deano: Early 20's, M

Mikey: Early 20's, M

The story is told from Ryan's point of view. The four main characters simultaneously play Ryan and in the case of Jason, Andy & Deano their own character when they are not speaking with Ryan's voice.

Please pay careful attention to the numbering of the roles as sometimes the running pattern of Ryan 1/2/3/4 is not always the same. This is intentional.

Mikey is seen but never heard and the role of Shanice or other characters can either be a voiceover or played by the actors in play as you see fit.

As you would expect, we encourage you to be as diverse in your casting as you are able.

A NOTE ON PLACE, TIME & SETTING

The show can be staged as simply as you like. We used 4 bright yellow folding chairs and lots of projection but you can stage the show as you see fit.

We used the idea of a "five-a-side" football team in terms of costume, with the characters names on the back, with shirts and ties for the funeral scene and the wake, and a "spare" shirt for Mikey.

Whilst the town which is the setting for the show is intended to suggest a town in the Midlands, you can either choose to set the show with actors of the same accent or different accents to reflect an "any town" feeling.

The transition between characters should be seamless and energetic and the audience should be used wherever possible to create interactions and fun moments. We really encourage you to fill the show with warmth, friendship, humour and life.

And finally, find a banging playlist of your favourite indie tunes and play it super loud.

See you on the dancefloor...

CONTENT ADVISORY

Flashbang contains very strong language, adult themes, discussion of sex & sexual activity, sudden loud noises, depictions of drugs & alcohol consumption, and discussions of grief, bereavement and mental health.

For more information, advice and support with any of the issues raised in this play, please visit **Samaritans** www.samaritans.org or the **Campaign Against Living Miserably (CALM)** www.thecalmzone.net

POWER RANGERS

Projection, back wall. A photo of five small boys (in school uniform?) fades in over the next sequence. They are aged about 6 or 7. Best Friends.

The four actors play simultaneously both RYAN, the main narrator of the story, and the three other boys in the photo and other characters as required. All standing in front of that photo. Undeniably the same group of mates.

RYAN 1 – PLAYS RYAN

RYAN 2 – ALSO PLAYS JASON

RYAN 3 – ALSO PLAYS ANDY

RYAN 4 – ALSO PLAYS DEANO.

Italics denote either speech directed to another person or a stress of those words.

PRESET: At the director's discretion.

RYAN 1: I never had a brother. I've got a sister, *absolute fucking nightmare*, and then there's Mum, Dad and Me.

Just your typical nuclear family, really, and by nuclear I don't mean my Mum when she gets pissed off at my Dad.

RYAN 4: And we're alright, and that – but there were always times when I was younger when I wondered what life would be like if I wasn't their only son.

RYAN 2: But to be honest, I might not have been lucky enough to have a proper brother, you know, like a biological one, but I reckon I've got the next best thing.

And he indicates the other three boys and the photo on the wall.

RYAN 3: Always had this lot to keep me company.

Now, don't tell them I told you, but I reckon they're alright, in their own bonkers way. If you'd have said we'd still be mates in our twenties from the look of this photo I'd say you were insane.

He looks up at the picture, sort of embarrassed.

RYAN 4: Fuck me, what a picture.

The others chip in.

RYAN 2: This is mortifying. Mate, what are you doing?

RYAN 3: Properly awkward, this is –

RYAN 4: – At least we know whose Mum still cuts their hair.

RYAN 1: Could be worse, although sometimes I wonder. We're just these lads from this small town in the middle of nowhere. One of those places you see on a road sign when you're driving on the motorway but you're never going to visit.

RYAN 2: Best way to describe where we live is that it's this little grey city 20 miles from anywhere important. 300,000 people and nothing ever happens.

Like ever.

RYAN 3: A place you could live your whole life in with houses that look almost identical. Semi-detached roads with Peugeots and Vauxhall Astras lined up in their hundreds.

RYAN 4: Tiny bits of grass lawn visible from space.

RYAN 3: It's this handful of neighbourhoods broken up by housing estates and some car parks orbiting a concrete shopping centre. White vans and industrial estates.

RYAN 1: And just like us, our parents grew up here too. Starting every day with the same ten -minute drive to work, doing the same standard job day in, day out year after year.

RYAN 2: My Mum and Dad, *Julie and Nigel*, got married to the first person they'd ever slept with. Spending every year since having kids, fish and chips on a Friday and saving to go on Thomson holiday to Majorca every summer – That's literally all they do.

RYAN 1: You look at old photos and it's all big peach bridesmaids dresses, Jules and Big Nige slow dancing to Wet Wet Wet and watching Blind Date on a Saturday Night. Their idea of a wild night out now is the salad bar at the Harvester up the road.

RYAN 4: Mate your Dad's definition of excited is when there's a new episode of Top Gear on the telly.

RYAN 3: Everyone knows everyone else's business, right? Like a shitty, more boring suburban version of *Eastenders*.

RYAN 4: And everything we think we've done first, they've done it all before us, just in more flammable fabrics and bigger hair.

RYAN 1: Birthday parties. Barbecues. Playing round each other's houses when we were kids. This place is just like a cycle that just keeps repeating itself from one generation to the next.

RYAN 2: Look, I'm not joking. The most important thing that happened to us where we lived was when the local football team made it to the playoffs of the League that year and everyone got to go to Wembley for the match.

RYAN 3: Says something that the most exciting things that happened here happened somewhere else. Right?

RYAN 4: We weren't ever going to be famous for anything. Nobody was ever going to write a story about us were they?

Choose your favourite word. Go on…

He points at the others, egging them on.

RYAN 1: Er… Boring?

RYAN 2: Safe.

RYAN 3: Yeah it really is a bit of a shithole in the middle of nowhere to be honest.

RYAN 2: Ah come on mate, that's not fair.

Hands up. Just telling the truth.

RYAN 3: Just telling it like it is.

RYAN 1: Sometimes, to keep things interesting, there'll be some big family drama or whatever, like when my mate Danny's Mum and Dad got divorced or the time Katie Morris's Dad won 50k on the Lottery and bought himself a Porsche and just like, fucked off –

RYAN 4: – Yeah but Katie Morris's Dad was a knob before he won the 50K so –

Cuts him off.

RYAN 1: – So anyway, stuff like that. Normal stuff.

RYAN 2: We're like real people. We're not people that grow up and move to other places. London people, whatever.

We don't do that sort of thing.

RYAN 4: Nothing wrong with being normal though. Is there?

About Deano.

RYAN 3: I assume we're not including Deano in that description of normal though right?

Deano fires right back, refers to the photo.

RYAN 4: No but seriously mate, what is going on with your hair in that photo?

RYAN 3: Yeah alright mate. Stop being a twat.

RYAN 1: Anyway… When we were kids, like 5 or 6, about the time someone took that photo, we did that thing that all kids do in primary school when they think that they're "well cool" or whatever.

There's a collective groan from the four of them.

RYAN 2: Oh Mate – You do know that saying "well cool" like that makes it the least cool thing ever. Right?

RYAN 1: Shut up, yeah of course I do.

RYAN 2: OK, Just checking.

RYAN 4: Are you *really* going to tell this story?

RYAN 1: Yeah course. Why not?

RYAN 4: Because it's embarrassing?

RYAN 1: No it's not!

RYAN 3: Yeah mate, sorry but it's actually shameful. I can guarantee nobody here wants to hear this story.

RYAN 1: No it's not shameful, don't be a dick.

Anyway...

Like he's confiding a secret.

So don't judge us right, But we started... *a gang*.

RYAN 4: Fuck's sake Ryan.

RYAN 2: He's doing it – he's actually doing it.

RYAN 3: You can't do this.

He carries on, smiling.

RYAN 1: Yeah, a gang! Look I'm owning it! Now we thought we were the best thing you'd seen since the Power Rangers were on telly – and let's be honest, that's the coolest thing you could be when you're six.

RYAN 3: Can we please not mention the fact we could also only be the Power Rangers because we had to include your little sister so she could be the pink one. Yeah?

RYAN 1: And all that was fine or whatever until Mrs. Harris, our Year 1 teacher told us that we weren't allowed to call ourselves a "gang" because gangs weren't very nice, so we had to say we were in a "group" instead.

RYAN 4: Ah fuck me, I remember this now. Wasn't she the one with the like Lego hair, yeah?

RYAN 2: Yep. Lego hair and really strong perfume? Oh yeah I remember her, holy water in her desk –

RYAN 3: We went to like the most uneventful Catholic primary school in the city and she's worrying that we're going to go all Peaky Blinders on her.

RYAN 1: Now don't get me wrong, but I don't see the X-Men or whatever describing themselves as a "group" now. Do you?

Even at the age of 6 that was properly *not* a cool way to describe ourselves.

RYAN 3: We could be a Squad? Maybe? Team? No?

No Reply

Well, I suppose it's sort of context specific isn't it?

RYAN 2: Nah, we were always very definitely a gang, no matter what she said.

RYAN 4: And when you're six, your life's all about fighting monsters, swapping Pokémon cards, working out which WWE wrestler was the best, trying to climb that massive tree in the park...

RYAN 1: Even though Andy's Mum always made him go home at 8 O'clock.

RYAN 3: Fuck off, Ryan.

RYAN 1: Come on, it is actually funny though.

RYAN 3: Oh really. Do you want me to tell everyone about the time you nearly shat yourself on Nemesis at Alton Towers or shall I?

Andy and Jason do a terrible impression of Ryan on a rollercoaster having a horrible time.

RYAN 1: Now it's about the grown-up versions of that. The banter and the experiences you have with your mates might change, but your friendship stays the same. Doesn't it?

Changes the subject.

Ok, So seeing as though they're gonna chip in at some point I should probably introduce the members of our very own version of the Justice League.

Another Groan...

RYAN 2: I beg you. Please *never* call it that again.

The following is presented like a roll call. Each of them comes forward one by one.

RYAN 3: So this is *Jason*. Always getting properly involved with some girl or other, often more than one at the same time. The drama surrounding his love life was almost as spectacular as his ability to score a goal on the football pitch. His right foot might have put loads of his neighbour's windows in but the less we say about his left foot the better. Right Jase?

RYAN 2: At least I can hit the fucking ball, mate. There's a reason we always stick you in goal...

RYAN 3: Fair point.

RYAN 2: And him over there is *Andy*, although he's –

In a parody of Andy's Mum nagging...

RYAN 1,2,4: *Are you listening to me Andrew!!!*

RYAN 2: – to his Mum. Mad keen on his music. The worst person to have in charge of the playlist at a party. I'd be surprised if he wasn't deaf by the time he was 40.

Andy pulls his headphones down.

RYAN 3: Sorry what did you say?

RYAN 2: I said you agreed that you'd agreed to get everyone a round later when all this was finished. Yeah...

RYAN 3: Did I fuck.

Wait, I didn't. Did I?

Ryan shakes his head, laughing

RYAN 1: Then that one over there in the corner is Deano. Mad, crazy bastard. *Actually mental.* Sometimes I look at him and I wonder if there's actually some wiring in his brain missing.

You ever have one of those mates with a nickname and you sort of forget what their real name was? Well yeah, that was him. Right from an early age we all knew he was the devil incarnate.

RYAN 2: If there was a crazy scheme he'd be in the middle of it, somewhere. Chip shop dinners smuggled into school at lunchtime, climbing on the roof of a building just because he could. NEVER actually paid for the bus into town.

RYAN 3: That filthy smile of his got him into and out of trouble more times than I can count.

RYAN 1: He was like this *myth*, an urban legend passed around in dark corners and between people huddled on a dance floor somewhere. Deano walks into a room and you know you were going to have a brilliant time.

Some of the best nights out I've ever had have all been all his fault. WHAT a legend –

– And then there's…

And he runs out of energy, because he's hit the missing space where Mikey should be. Everything grinds to an awkward halt.

RYAN 3: Do we want to do this?

He looks at the others for reassurance. A beat, then someone says.

RYAN 2: Yeah go on.

RYAN 1: I think we should.

RYAN 4: Come on, don't be dickheads. I'll do it.

And he steps in.

RYAN 4: You see right, well, he's not here now, but at the end was Mikey. The smallest one. Youngest of this mad, massive Irish family. Three brothers and two sisters. Like the huge scary gangster family in Shameless, the ones you don't want to fuck about with.

RYAN 3: Hey, maybe that's why Mrs. Harris wouldn't let us be in a gang, in case we actually ended up handling stolen goods for Mikey's dodgy Uncle Sean?

RYAN 2: Yeah maybe you're right actually.

But of course that never happened, right?

They all look at Deano. Eyebrows raised.

RYAN 4: It was just that one time…

Besides, not like anyone got caught, is it?

They're not convinced. Moving on…

RYAN 1: The other problem with Mikey is that he was always injuring himself. Right liability. You could guarantee that if there was a wall to fall off, a football injury to be had, or someone to trip over their own feet, it would be him.

RYAN 4: The only kid I've ever known actually fall upstairs – Couldn't make it up.

RYAN 3: By the time he was 16 he'd probably broken most of the bones in his body.

RYAN 4: Well he was always going to end up in A&E wasn't he?

Ouch. He's hit something he shouldn't have. Everyone winces.

RYAN 2: Fuck's sake Deano. Did you have to? Don't be a prick.

RYAN 4: Sorry. I didn't mean it to come out like that.

Jason aggy – squaring up a bit.

RYAN 2: Yeah well engage your brain, just once, will you?

Calming them down.

RYAN 1: It's ok. We know what you meant, mate.

Don't be twats.

RYAN 2: Anyway. moving on, but he was like the clever one too right? Not conventionally clever, like I'd never be too sure whether I'd want to copy his exam results or whatever but like sensible. You know? The right answer for everything.

RYAN 3: Yeah, he was brilliant, but he always looked like he needed someone to look after him.

Pushes away a bad memory. Shakes it off. Someone nods at Ryan, urges him on.

RYAN 1: So I guess that just leaves me, and you know a bit about me already. I guess. I'm just normal, I think? Well I reckon I am anyway.

Teasing…

RYAN 3: Yeah you might think you're normal but we all know you put too much gel on your hair and you're always late for everything because you spend way too long in the bathroom and –

RYAN 1: – And I'm just living my life yeah. You know? Thank you, Mate.

Work, pub, sleep, repeat. No fucking idea what I wanted to do with my life. Crap job in a trainer shop in town. Still living with my Mum and Dad. Who gives a shit?

RYAN 2: And the years keep rolling by, one after the other.

RYAN 3: And those kids in the photo get older too.

RYAN 4: Rushing through that whole cycle of growing up together.

RYAN 1: Best of mates.

RYAN 2: Proper banter. In-jokes. Things only we understood.

RYAN 1: Trying to keep Deano out of trouble and Mikey out of A&E. Winding Andy up by telling him that the Arctic Monkeys are shite.

RYAN 3: Mate - your sister dragged you along to see Steps on tour last year so best we don't go there yeah?

Smiling. Banter. In the background someone mimes *"Tragedy"* at him, taking the piss.

RYAN 1: Yeah but the Arctic Monkeys are shite though.

RYAN 4: We were a gang, you know? Didn't matter what that teacher said. There was no other way of putting it.

RYAN 1: My squad and me. Best "group" of boys in the universe, we were.

Foreshadowing – like they know what's coming (and who's missing from the lineup.)

RYAN 2: Until everything changed and we weren't anymore.

TRANSITION

CALL OF DUTY

They change places. A different movement formation. They've warmed up a bit.

RYAN 1: Time flies. Doesn't it? One minute you're pretending to be Michael Owen in the playground and the next you're standing with your mates in a queue somewhere waiting to collect your GCSE results.

RYAN 2: Staring at some future point in time where you're supposed to have your life sorted, which is really pretty bleak actually because last time I checked the world was burning.

RYAN 3: Marking out periods of time in your life with moments in time and objects that you hang onto.

RYAN 4: School years. Swimming badges. Facebook statuses. Blurry photos from those four days you spent at Glastonbury last year or points on your driving licence because you passed your test first chance you could and caned it down the Eastern By-Pass a bit too quickly one day.

To someone else.

– I wasn't running from the police. Honest…

RYAN 1: And then there's all the other stuff. WhatsApp chats. In-jokes. Meme sharing. Making plans for Saturday night. Commiserating about bad dates like:

They've gradually started to move in to take the piss out of Jason.

RYAN 3: *"Oh mate I can't believe she binned you off like that"*

RYAN 1: or:

RYAN 4: *"I can't believe he missed that fucking penalty –"*

Jason gets his own back…

RYAN 2: Thinking "The Inbetweeners" is the funniest thing you've ever seen but secretly worrying that you relate too hard because it's basically your life.

RYAN 3: Shitting yourself that you've got no choices in life when in fact you know that you've got a pile of laundry that's been on your bedroom floor for 4 weeks and you can either take it to the machine in three minutes or you can sit down and play Call of Duty on the PlayStation for five hours instead.

RYAN 4: You can leave home, move into your own flat, and come back for Sunday dinner, or you can live at home and get your Mum to wake you up when you're late for work and get so pissed off with you procrastinating that she sticks your boxers in the washing machine herself

Much easier that way, I reckon.

RYAN 1: Now I don't know if I'm scared of the future or not. Some days I reckon I should break the fuck out of here and run away to London or whatever and other days I think I should accept it and realise that it's all been mapped out for me.

RYAN 1: Wife, Kids, Sunday League Football and one of those Semi-Detached houses with UPVC everywhere.

RYAN 2: And there's big things we should talk about. You know? Massive things. Important things. Things that we're scared of. Like, things you really want your mates to know because they're keeping you awake at night but you're worried you'll look like a dick if you tell them.

RYAN 3: Because it's way easier to laugh about that one time you stole a load of shopping trolleys and did a Grand Prix round the B&Q car park and it's way less painful than that dodgy tattoo you got on your 19th birthday on holiday because you were too drunk to remember your name so you got a permanent reminder in Chinese on your hip bone instead.

He winces, checks the tattoo.

RYAN 4: Fuck me, that tattoo hurt.

RYAN 1: We built our friendship on those experiences. Wordless connections between these kids who were making their way through life without a sat nav. So what do you do when you take a wrong turn?

Five car-pile up on the M6 that's what.

RYAN 2: Too busy living in this moment rather than planning for the next one.

RYAN 3: I wish I'd learned something from my Mum, or my sister or any one of those other brilliant women who always seemed to know what they were doing, even Andy's Mum who to be honest, and she's the most terrifying woman I've ever met.

Flashing Forward. Foreshadowing.

RYAN 4: Wish we hadn't left it so long to say what we felt. You know?

RYAN 1: Yeah. I wish I was braver about a lot of things.

RYAN 2: Do you think he knows?

RYAN 3: How could he not?

TRANSITION

HUGO BOSS

A big change of energy, ramping up for a big night out. Music, lights, an outside queue gives way to the dancefloor of a local nightclub...

RYAN 2: There's one thing I do know for sure though right. No matter where you are in the country on any given Saturday night, you find it's the same wherever you go.

RYAN 3: It's like this ritual. That whole process of getting ready to go out. Spending an hour in the shower and trying to get your hair "just right". Finding the whitest pair of "smart" trainers you own and hoping that there's a clean shirt in the wardrobe.

RYAN 1: Few quick pints in Wetherspoons to get things going. Waiting for that one mate that's always late.

That means you Deano.

RYAN 4: And you know that every town's got a nightclub like ours. The only one in the city which stays open till three am and forms the backdrop to some of the best nights of your life, and some you'd rather forget.

RYAN 1: It doesn't matter that they're all rotting old cinemas with shit names ripped off from 1980's porn palaces –

RYAN 2: It doesn't matter that you're one hundred percent sure the toilet attendant hates you and

	that by 1 am there'll be sweat running down the walls –
RYAN 3:	It doesn't matter that you stick to the carpet which might once have been purple (or is it orange?) and is now some weird shade of brown instead.
RYAN 4:	*Fucking genius*, all of it.
RYAN 1:	I'd love to say that it was difficult, like we had to try really hard and smuggle ourselves in like we were in Ocean's Eleven or whatever but the bouncers never gave a shit.

Jason, front of the queue, staring down a big scary bouncer...

RYAN 2:	Do the right things. Don't be a twat. Wear the right shoes. Don't talk back to the big scary fucker on the door and everything will be fine. Do it right and you just get waved right through.
RYAN 3:	And you get inside and the air is thick with music and people shouting. Dancing. Swaying about. Pressing themselves up against each other.
RYAN 4:	And then you're in the middle of this swirling mass of people. Sharing this experience with all these people weekend after weekend.
RYAN 1:	Crap commercial dance music in one room, R&B in the other, and a shitload of drunk people

littering the corridors. People Spilling out onto the street fighting, shouting, being sick.

RYAN 2: And we never just went out, we went *"out, out"* if you know what I mean. No point in doing things by halves.

RYAN 3: And in the midst of those lights flashing and that music pumping you could either get involved or stand and watch it happen. It was ours, just for us and just for the weekend.

RYAN 4: The air is this cloud of perfume and hair gel and Hugo Boss and haze from the machine by the DJ, and the steam and sweat and lust from all these people all sort of mixes together in this cocktail you could get drunk from just from breathing it in.

RYAN 1: Best time is just before midnight, when you're just drunk enough to enjoy it but not so drunk that you pass out. Waving your arms in the air because *you don't give a shit*.

RYAN 2: Shouting at your mates over the sound of the music and nobody can hear what you're saying anyway because it doesn't fucking matter mate, not one bit.

RYAN 3: Catching someone's eye, hoping you'll see them later but knowing in an hour they'll be copping off with someone else.

RYAN 4: Sometimes I'd just find a spot on the balcony overlooking the dancefloor, just to stand and watch. Everyone ends up splitting off, doing their own thing.

And it always goes a little something like this:

The music and energy changes to allow for the five of them doing different things in different sections of the nightclub.

RYAN 1: Jason makes a beeline for some girl. Turns out she's a mate of his sisters and she's been trying to set them up for ages. I know that he's onto a losing streak because I've already seen her trying to kop off with one of the bouncers and that's a high stakes game he stands no chance of winning.

RYAN 2: Andy's in the corner somewhere pretending like this is all above him and that he absolutely hates everyone and everything. In fact, what you need to understand about Andy is that if he's two cans of Red Stripe in and Dizzee Rascal comes on, you'll find him dancing like a twat just like everyone else.

RYAN 3: Never said I was responsible for what I did when I get drunk, did I?

RYAN 1: Somewhere, usually in the middle of it all, waving his arms round his head like weird fucking octopus is Deano. No fear, no regrets. He's got this gift, talks to anyone. If he formed a religion I'd hold out my hand and be like "sign me up". Course knowing Deano we'd end up getting kidnapped or something? Be fun to find out though. *Absolute legend.*

RYAN 4: And it's all good. You Know? Getting rid of the hopes and fears of the week with £2 Jaeger Bombs and drowning yourself in vodka sprayed at you from a water pistol from some girl who is way out of your fucking league.

RYAN 1: I look up, and in the corner, Mikey's leaning on the wall watching. Always checking his phone because he knows he'll get into trouble from his girlfriend if he gets home in a state.

RYAN 2: And he never does. Well not often, anyway.

RYAN 3: And you might think that it's all "lads, lads, lads" or whatever but it wasn't like that, not all the time. Just some nights. The mental ones. Those nights were *fucking brilliant.*

RYAN 4: Judge us if you want, because we were just getting on with it – living our lives and making the best of it.

RYAN 1: Living for the weekend. The summit of this mountain you spent the whole week climbing – our very own Mount Kilimanjaro.

RYAN 3: *Hang on do you even know where Mount Kilimanjaro is?*

RYAN 1: *Mate I have got no fucking idea!*

RYAN 2: And there's some nights I pull, and some nights I don't – and some nights I don't care. Because I

> know the universe gives with one hand and takes away with another. And the best thing about living with your parents is that you're not paying rent so you might as well get the fuck on with it because you can't spend it when you're dead, can you?

Some throw forward here to Mikey, Like a focus pull. Some sort of foreshadowing.

RYAN 3: You don't have long to wonder what you're doing with your life, because before you have time to think someone grabs you and drags you back to the dancefloor and you end up bouncing up and down with your shirt off to some stupid David Guetta song with your best mates.

They end up throwing themselves into it as the lights power down. End of the night...

RYAN 4: It gets late, that midnight energy starts to slide into the 2am slump, and we're just swaying around as the night begins to die out. People drift away and flag down cabs home, and we start the usual routine of trying to see if we've got enough cash to join them so we don't have to walk 5 miles home.

RYAN 1: Everyone does their own thing. Jason cops off with some random girl, not the girl he was after earlier. Deano ends up at some house party God knows where, and the rest of us end up walking home trying to make sure Mikey doesn't get into trouble.

The dancefloor's given way to neon strip lights and bleary eyes. A kebab shop.

RYAN 2: Always ends up with us outside the kebab shop on the way home. Sitting on the pavement sharing a bag of chips with the last of the money we've scraped together as the sun comes up.

Self-Aware.

RYAN 3: Look, I'm never going to be one of those lads that packs everything in and moves to a bigger city. I'm just not. I know that this is where I belong and where I'm going to stay.

RYAN 4: But it's nights like that, when I wake up on one of my mate's sofas and I can't remember half of what we got up in the hours before that I'll treasure when I'm old.

RYAN 1: We were never going to change the world. I wasn't going to be a Doctor, or a Lawyer, or win Love Island or whatever. I was just going to be this lad that was going to get on with it and live his life. You know?

RYAN 2: I had my mates with me, and we were enough.

RYAN 4: We were always going to be enough.

TRANSITION

HAPPY NEW YEAR!

Back Projection: One year earlier. New Year's Eve. The four boys in the middle of a New Year's Countdown. Party vibe – get the audience involved etc. Party hats and beer. A real sense of celebration in the air. "Come on, it's about to start" etc...

RYAN 1,3,4: TEN!

Something's pulled Jason out of the party, like he's watching the whole thing back through time.

JASON: It's New Year's Eve, and everyone's piled into my living room, just like every year. We've always done it. Like it's a tradition. We go to Ryan's in the summer for a big barbecue but New Year's is our turn.

My Mum goes absolutely fucking mental over the buffet, like proper fucking mental. Sends me and my Dad to Iceland to go out and do a smash and grab to buy as much frozen party food as she can.

And every year we're like "Mum, just leave it, people just want to eat a few bits and have a drink, stop worrying." And every year she's like *"I am not having a house full of people and just feeding them sausages Jason"*

Now I don't want to say she's in competition with Ryan's Mum but there's definitely a rivalry there somewhere. So she spends three days cooking and everyone else basically gets wasted and ends up going home with boxes of

Tupperware packed with leftovers because she insists, and let's face it - nobody's messing with her when she's got an idea in her head.

RYAN 1,3,4: NINE!

JASON: And over the years we've gone from playing with the toys we got for Xmas for sneaking in one glass of wine to bottles of cheap fizz from M&S because Mum gets sophisticated at Christmas. And every year we're all together all of us – all our families get together with our neighbours seeing off the year. Waiting for Big Ben & the fireworks.

RYAN 1,2,3,4: EIGHT!

JASON: Looking back at all those years. The five of us. Getting on, getting older. This time next year I'll have a car, or this year we're going on holiday. Gonna get my coaching certificate, Finally get off with Katie Morris. Whatever.

And every year, just before midnight, my Dad barrels through the room telling everyone to charge their glasses and make their resolutions. Spilling prosecco on the carpet. "Look back and kiss the year goodbye everybody, it won't ever be here again!"

RYAN 1,2,3,4: SEVEN!

JASON: And we never talked about we wished for, well because it wouldn't come true then, would it?

But you had to wonder right, what those five boys wished for every New Year's Eve.

RYAN 1,2,3,4: SIX!

JASON: Flashing back through the year to all your best bits and looking forward to the future. Like when someone got evicted from Big Brother and they showed all those clips of everything you did – little snippets of all the highs and lows in one greatest hits package.

RYAN 1,2,3,4: FIVE!

JASON: And they're always really special, those parties. I dunno why. It just felt like for one night of the year everyone you ever loved was in one place. Banter, laughter, singing along to "Come on Eileen". Nobody worrying or fighting. Doing what we did best.

RYAN 1,2,3,4: FOUR!

And the momentum shifts.

JASON: Last year though. Weird year. Last year it was different, and I don't know why. Like I looked at them all and something didn't feel right. We're counting down to midnight and I look across the room. For one split second I catch Mikey across the room. Frozen in that one second. We're all happy and laughing and dancing and there's this look on his face I can't place. It's like he knows that this is the year. Next year's going to be different.

Beat.

> And he's smiling, but I get this feeling I can't shake, like a premonition that something bad's gonna happen.

Awkward. It's weird.

> It's like the world's about to change and you're not quite sure you're ready for what's coming next.

> And he smiles, looks me dead in the face and says:

> *This year mate, it's going to be the best year yet. I know it. Just you wait and see!*

JASON: What do you say to that? Probably just me being stupid. I've drunk too much, too bloody emotional - pick an excuse. I'm just being stupid. Whatever. It's nothing.

Pause.

> So I do that thing you always do when you're hiding what you feel from your best mate.

> I tell him a lie instead.

Laughs it off. Unconvincingly.

> "Course it is mate – it's going to be brilliant."

And it's like time stops. As they all start celebrating around him he looks back at them as time speeds up again. There's a beat – a moment of realisation.

RYAN 1,2,3,4: Three! Two! One! Happy New Year!

And they're celebrating, fireworks, party poppers, Auld Lang Syne, Big Ben confetti. And they catch Jason and drag him back into the party as the light changes – but he knows there's something not quite right as the light changes.

TRANSITION

BABY PHOTO

A Phone lights up in the middle of the stage. WhatsApp message.

RYAN 1: It came out of the blue.

RYAN 2: Friday night. Message on our WhatsApp group. Mikey.

Now normally it's just text speak and far too many emojis. But this time he just gets straight to the point.

RYAN 3: *Hey Mate. Where R U?*

RYAN 1: I'm the first to reply.

RYAN 2: *I'm at home. What's up?*

RYAN 3: *I'm @ Siobhan's. Come over. Need 2 tlk to U.*

RYAN 4: Now usually it's because there's been some disaster and his leg is hanging off or whatever but the fact he's texting and not calling is a bit weird.

RYAN 1: *Where's Leanne?*

Cuts in.

RYAN 2: We should probably explain that Leanne's Mikey's girlfriend, right?

Something's happened in the past between Deano and Leanne. He cuts in.

RYAN 4: God, she's so annoying. Fuck Leanne, man.

RYAN 2: Leave it Deano – Go on mate.

RYAN 3: *@ her Mum's. Will explain when U get here.*

RYAN 1: I check the time on my phone and it's 9.30. Planned on staying in and playing Fifa in bed and I don't know if I can really be arsed to go out again, but the others say they're going over too, so I throw on a hoodie and some trainers and head for the bus stop.

RYAN 2: Siobhan's Mikey's sister – she lives in this old council block on the way into town. She'd gone to Ireland to see their Nan for two weeks, and they'd sometimes let Mikey house-sit, which is braver than I'd ever be.

RYAN 3: And of course she lives on the Twenty-Fifth Fucking Floor and the lift's busted, so I have to practically *shove* Jason and Deano up the stairs, whingeing about how they should have stayed at home instead.

RYAN 4: I catch the light through the window in the stairwell, and it's one of those perfect summer evenings, you know? where it's like 10 o'clock at night but it's still not dark outside yet.

RYAN 2: Funny how you remember the weird little details about a night like that. Just remember the sky being this funny blue / orange colour, like it was wrong.

RYAN 1: We get to the flat and Mikey is standing on the balcony, just looking into town as the sunlight is dying and he's got this sort of weird, happy smile on his face.

RYAN 2: At least he hasn't burnt the flat down or killed someone – so that's a good start.

RYAN 4: Alright then mate, are you going to tell us why you're being so weird?

RYAN 3: I'm not being weird.

RYAN 1: He says – And I realise that he's actually really sort of self-conscious – he'd always been a bit awkward but this was something else.

RYAN 3: There's just something I wanted to tell you. Well – show you really.

RYAN 1: He looks over, and reaches into the pocket of his jeans and pulls out this piece of paper.

He reaches into his pocket and pulls out a crumpled and folded piece of paper.

RYAN 4: I open it, and I know straight away what it is. It's this crumpled, black and white picture of a scan.

RYAN 3: A scan of a baby.

RYAN 2: His Baby.

RYAN 1: And everything goes quiet as we all pass it round just sort of staring at it.

RYAN 2: I wanted to tell you in person. Didn't seem right to send a text. Found out this morning.

>   Leanne... Leanne's having a baby.

RYAN 4: I'm going to be a Dad.

There is a stunned silence for a second as it sinks in…

RYAN 1: Of all the things I thought might happen tonight this is definitely not one of them.

Hold…

> There's this split second where we're all silent. Like mouth-open shocked. And we're all waiting for someone to be the first person to react. We're all just looking at him, and this picture and that smile on his face and then it all makes sense.

RYAN 2: *Fuck.*

RYAN 4: *Mate.*

RYAN 3: And then, just like scoring a winning goal at Wembley in the 92nd minute of extra time we all go *mad*. Cheering and jumping up and down and shouting, smacking him on the back and telling him how brilliant it was.

RYAN 4: A Baby. An actual real life kid. One of us was going to be a Dad and weirdest of all it was the lad that couldn't look after himself, let alone another tiny human.

Fuck me, the universe is *weird*.

RYAN 1: Didn't even matter that we'd always found Leanne to be a bit of a pain in the arse to be honest because this was *brilliant*, it absolutely was.

RYAN 2: There were a hundred questions, course there were. Were they going to keep it? *(Yes they were...)* Were they going to move out and get a place of their own? *(Yes they were).* Was his Mum angry? *(Yes but his Mum was always angry so nothing had changed there.)*

RYAN 4: *Most importantly. Were they going to name it after Deano?*

Everyone stops and looks at him. Absolutely not.

RYAN 1: NO Deano. They're not going to name it after you. Not under any circumstances..

RYAN 4: Worth a try. Second Name?

RYAN 1,2,3: *NO!*

RYAN 3: And as we're all standing there, I realise Mikey is the happiest I've seen him in his entire life. It's mind blowing to me that soon everything is going to change forever. He's only gone and done it – bagged himself a girlfriend and a kid and that's absolutely brilliant. Isn't it?

RYAN 4: If that were me I'd be fucking terrified, but he doesn't seem to be that worried. All I can see is him standing on this balcony with the sun going down behind us clutching this piece of paper with this weird, grainy alien-baby photo of his little girl on it.

RYAN 1: We're growing up – it's finally happening. There's a brand new Pink Power Ranger to join our squad and that's everything he ever wanted.

RYAN 2: And then, after the shock and the cheering died down you know what happened next.

RYAN 4: We fucking celebrated - Course we did!

RYAN 1: Someone digs out a Spotify playlist from a random iPhone and Deano (resourceful as ever) produces a box of beers and two bottles of vodka. Mikey swears it wasn't Siobhan's so who knows where it came from – I've learned to stop asking, life's easier that way.

RYAN 4: We're singing along to "Feel the Love" by Rudimental. Stupid dancing on the roof, bouncing up and down. Congratulating him over and over again and telling him all the ridiculous amounts of trouble that baby is going to get into when we're allowed to babysit

RYAN 1: And I feel it too. You know? Life's not going to be the same any more, it's going to be so much better than that.

RYAN 2: The old lady next door bangs the walls and tells us to *keep it down*, and some bloke riding on a bike downstairs looks up to see what the noise is all about.

RYAN 3: *I'm having a kid!* Mikey yells, looking down at him. *I'm gonna be a Dad and it's going to be fucking brilliant!*

RYAN 4: He's just made up. You know? It's infectious, that sort of happiness. The guy downstairs throws him this massive smile and a thumbs up as he rides off into the distance.

RYAN 1: It should have been perfect, all of us celebrating like that on that balcony. One more photo to add to all those photos of the five of us over the years.

There's a shift, something changes. He appears confused.

> I don't know what happened next. I guess we were all too wound up to be paying attention properly. It's like when you're riding down a hill on your bike and you're not sure if your brakes are gonna work.

RYAN 2: Maybe we all should have paid more attention, because in the middle of all that fucking joy we all did that thing we hadn't done for years, and that was take our eye off Mikey in case he hurt himself…

RYAN 3: And we're all laughing, and dancing, and singing, looking out twenty five floors up over this city where nothing ever happened…

RYAN 4: And those old flats? Guess they weren't as safe as they are now. Guess Mikey wasn't paying attention either.

And now something's gone very horribly wrong…

RYAN 1: Nobody really noticed that he'd leant out over the rail at the balcony to cheer at that guy downstairs.

RYAN 2: Nobody really noticed that the wind caught that crumpled up scan of his baby and blew it out of his hand –

RYAN 3: Nobody really noticed that he'd leant over a bit more to try and catch that photo of his baby girl before it blew away –

RYAN 4: But all of us definitely noticed when he overbalanced and fell off the balcony of that tower block from the Twenty Fifth Floor…

There is a pause, a hold, a deep inhalation of breath as the lights go down and their whole lives change forever…

TRANSITION

FLASHBANG

As the lights come up the equation for terminal velocity appears on the back wall.

The sound of an insistent ticking.

Mikey is falling. The others frozen in place.

RYAN 1: Never paid attention in science lessons. Waste of time. Was never going to leave school and become a nuclear physicist, was I?

RYAN 4: Periodic table's a piece of furniture you get out one in a while when you have Sunday dinner, isn't it?

RYAN 2: One night last week though, I actually googled this on my phone. Don't know why.

RYAN 3: Did it help?

RYAN 4: Did it fuck.

They all take out their phones and read. Scientist-like.

RYAN 1: The terminal velocity of a falling body occurs during free fall when the force due to gravity is exactly balanced by the force due to air resistance, such that the body experiences zero acceleration. The formula for terminal velocity (where buoyancy in air is negligible) is given by the thrust. Where –

RYAN 2: *m is the mass of the falling object –*

RYAN 3:   *g is the acceleration due to gravity (9.8 meters squared)* –

RYAN 4:   *Cd is the drag coefficient (roughly 0.7 for head down position, roughly 1 for belly-to-earth position)*

RYAN 1:   *ρ is the density of the fluid through which the object is falling (1.23 kg per meter cubed for air at sea level, and roughly 0.99 kg per meter cubed at the middle of the measurement zone (Two thousand two hundred metres)*

RYAN 2:   *A is the projected area of the object, or area cross-section (roughly 0.18 metres squared for head down position, roughly 0.7 for belly-to-earth position)*

RYAN 3:   *So, for a human in belly-to-earth position ($A = 0.7$ metres squared, $m = 90$ kg, $Cd = 1$) this gives 50.6 metres per second, about the terminal velocity of the typical skydiver of 55 metres per second.*

With a slam over each of the following lines the real world thunders back in.

RYAN 4:   I'm standing there, on that balcony, just watching him disappear over the edge.

RYAN 3:   ...And all I can see is his face. The look of absolute shock in his eyes as he goes.

Slam.

RYAN 1:   It's like we're all frozen. All the air and the sound and the energy has gotten sucked out of the freezing cold night and taken him with it.

Another slam over the word §flashbang§ below.

RYAN 2: This fucking *flashbang* has gone off in my face. Ringing in my ears as he vanishes into the black.

RYAN 3: It's like I'm watching this happen to some stranger. Someone else. It's like I'm outside my body as he's hurtling to earth off the twenty-fifth floor of this building.

RYAN 4: Except he's not just some random stranger, is he? It's not happening to someone else.

RYAN 1: Nah, He's not flying. Flying's a good thing. A happy thing. Flying implies there's some choice in the matter.

Nah, Mikey is falling –

RYAN 2: Falling through the air like a missile – hurtling towards the ground at Fifty metres a second.

RYAN 3: There's nothing to break his fall.

RYAN 4: And there's nothing we can do about it.

Another slam over the word snaps below as real life starts to crash in around them. Back to real time...

RYAN 1: And then it's like the rubber band *snaps* back and all the air and the sound rushes back in and time catches up with the world again just before he hits the ground.

And they rush to the edge, as if to look down.

RYAN 2: Oh *shit*. Fucking hell.

Pause.

RYAN 3: Jesus. Like we have to do something. Call for help or something?

Jason, shouting downwards, over the edge…

RYAN 2: Mate. Can you hear me?

RYAN 4: *He obviously can't hear you, can he, Dickhead!?*

RYAN 3: What can we do – what the hell are we going to do? Maybe call an ambulance or something?

RYAN 2: There's nothing we can do.

RYAN 3: Somebody has to do something!

RYAN 4: It's 20 floors down, mate.

RYAN 2: Shit.

And they all look on at Ryan, who is frozen in terror.

RYAN 3: *Ryan fucking do something!* –

Another slam. Bigger this time, and the stage is smashed into a blackout.

There's just the sound or an urgent ticking, which comes to a definitive stop as time runs out.

RYAN 1: *Fuck…*

BLACKOUT

NEWS BOOK

Change of energy. Starker, colder. A police station interview room in the middle of the night.

A neon light fires...

RYAN 1: Every Monday morning when we were kids we used to have to write down everything we'd done at the weekend for the teacher to read. Like a news book thing.

RYAN 2: I dunno whether they were looking for any juicy gossip or whatever, maybe they were spying on us, I dunno. Sometimes they might have got the occasional drunk fight between parents or whatever but mostly I reckon it was just kids talking about how they'd gone to Asda and ate McDonald's with a load of badly drawn pictures of people with sticks for arms and massive lollipop heads.

RYAN 1: Mikey and me went to play round Jason's house.

RYAN 3: When you get older - you don't look at the world like a kid would any more. There's all sorts of different words to describe the horrendous things that happen to grown-ups.

RYAN 2: Mikey fell off his bike and hurt his arm.

RYAN 4: Harder words, colder ones. Technical descriptions of people, events and places to describe the things that happen that you can't soften, no matter how hard you try.

RYAN 1: *Toxicology Reports.*

RYAN 2: *Mortuary Access.*

RYAN 3: *Blood Alcohol Levels.*

RYAN 4: *Impact trajectory.*

RYAN 1: *Witness Statements.*

RYAN 4: *Dead on arrival.*

RYAN 2: *Post Mortem. Fuck's sake...*

RYAN 3: The usual. Police interviews, autopsy reports, all that shit. Mikey's Mum losing her shit at some poor nurse when she was asked if they wanted to donate his organs and his Dad squaring up to Jason in the corridor.

RYAN 2: Sitting in separate rooms in the middle of the night trying to prove on a tape recording that we didn't kill him on purpose.

RYAN 1: Some of those police officers were alright, you know? Nice, almost.

RYAN 3: Some of them were less good about it. Like they didn't give a shit what a tragic accident it was – just wanted to go home. Get it over with.

RYAN 1: Stupid lads that should have known better that have gone and got their mate killed.

RYAN 4: I'm sitting there while this copper is talking absolute shite watching this clock on the wall

	counting out the hours. Every time it ticks it's like being stabbed in the chest.
RYAN 1:	Thinking about how just a few hours before the world seemed like such a different place.
RYAN 2:	Hangover wears off pretty quickly.
	Shattered in more ways than one.
RYAN 3:	Shock sets in. It's cold and dark – the electric lights make everyone look terrible.
RYAN 1:	And Mikey's in the back of some ambulance somewhere with a sheet over his face.

The passage of time.

RYAN 4:	I guess in the end they concluded it was an accident or whatever and once they'd taken everyone's statements we were free to go. Handing everything over to the coroner.

Free to go, just like that…

RYAN 1:	My Dad comes and takes me home and in the car home I realise I can't stop shaking.
RYAN 2:	There's so many things I could tell you Mikey and his life. You know? About that night, about the crazy things we got up to. The things nobody will ever write about in a news book and the things none of <u>you</u> will ever know about him
RYAN 3:	*Age 6 – "We went to the cinema to watch Shrek – I had a large popcorn and a Blueberry Ice Blast"*

RYAN 4: Age 13 – "We went to Mikey's birthday party at the Laser Quest in town."

RYAN 2: Age 18 – "Just got back from this mental week in Faliraki. Lost Mikey on the strip AGAIN. Seven whole days of getting wankered in the sunshine. Who's idea was that stupid tattoo?!"

RYAN 1: Nah, he's not coming out tonight, he's going on a date with Leanne instead.

RYAN 3: And then this year:

In the style of an official report. Deano is a mean copper leaning into Ryan's face.

RYAN 4: "Subject is a 24 year old male who fell from a balcony at a height of above 20 floors as a result of impaired judgement likely due to excessive alcohol consumption. Massive internal injuries with death likely to be instantaneous upon impact at ground level…"

RYAN 1: Everything summed up in one brutal line.

RYAN 2: Death by Misadventure.

RYAN 3: And what's that then?

Back in the style of the report. Deano the mean copper again.

RYAN 4: *Misadventure is a legally defined manner of death: a way by which an actual cause of death (trauma, exposure, etc.) was allowed to occur. For example, a death caused by an illicit drug overdose may be* *ruled a death by misadventure, as the user took the risk of drug usage voluntarily.*

RYAN 3: Right.

RYAN 1: You know what, calling it "misadventure" is actually a really fucking cold way to describe the way someone died, you know? *Prick*.

RYAN 2: The way *he*, died, you mean?

RYAN 3: Don't word it like he did it on purpose. That's not right, that isn't.

RYAN 4: Not his fault he fell off, is it?

RYAN 1: And allowed it to happen? Nah Mate. I never allowed anything to happen and neither did they.

RYAN 2: If you asked me now I'd still say if there was anything to do to make it better then I would. No matter what you or his girlfriend or anyone else with an opinion might scream at us across the living room of someone's house or in the supermarket.

RYAN 3: But if you think I'd "allow" one of my best mates to die like that? It's fucking tragic that is. It eats me alive every day. So if you think that there was anyway I'd just stand back and "let" this happen, then you know what you can do, right?

RYAN 4: You can get to fuck.

A door slams somewhere and the world has changed forever.

TRANSITION

TUBTHUMPING

Andy. Bloody nose, black eye. Fighting his way out of his problems. He looks at his phone.

ANDY: Fuck's sake.

Tries to wipe the blood from his nose.

> Remember that song? The Chumbawamba song. You know the one I mean – The stupid "I get knocked down, but I get up again." one. Used to play it all the time when we were kids - all these 7 year olds jumping up and down not really knowing what they were singing about but loving it anyway. Birthday parties, School Discos, Leanne Morris's 16th birthday party when her Dad hired that bloke to DJ who later got done for owning a cannabis farm.
>
> Anyway. Mikey fucking loved that song. Like properly loved it. Even when we were older and they used to play it sometimes you'd find him in the corner somewhere just sort of like moving his arms around.
>
> Flailing about like some sort of carrier bag in the wind – it was like his anthem or something.

Laughs, genuinely.

> Yeah. The kid that always got back up again.
>
> I was never really that bothered about school stuff. Always half fancied doing something else, like opening up a music studio or a record shop

or whatever. Try and educate this stupid little town about proper music. Like there's more to life than Calvin Fucking Harris. Know what I mean?

And Mikey, well we always said we'd do it together. Because I'm telling you – He was smarter than most people gave him credit for. Was just never going to shout about it.

We used to disappear to gigs in Birmingham without telling the others sometimes, just to do something a bit different. Used to talk on the bus on the way back about how we'd set up a business. *Do something together. "You've just got to have a plan, mate"* – he'd say. *"Go on Dragon's Den."* Face in a cheap burger with his feet on the seats, because yeah, that's exactly the sort of thing Deborah Meaden would give her money to.

And now...

Well now that idea's fucked. Isn't it? Because instead of sneaking off and leaving Jason and Deano playing FIFA or whatever they used to do on a Thursday night I'm on my own getting off my face wondering what might have been. Aren't I?

Pause. Thinks a bit

> Here's what I know, right? It's not about getting knocked down and getting back up

> again, is it? It's about all the other things. Going out, getting fucked up, bouncing off the walls. Finding the biggest fucker you can find in a club somewhere and picking a fight with them in the hope that they smack you in the face.
>
> And I dunno why I'm doing it, if I'm honest. Because it never worked for him so why should it work for me? Except that I'm probably much more fucking angry and hurt and maybe if someone punches me in the face it might knock some sense into me, or something...

Self-Aware.

> I appreciate this is 100 percent the opposite of having a plan by the way...

Pause. Let it sit.

> Here's the thing though. You fall over and you dust yourself off and you'll be fine. You know somehow you're going to be able to pick yourself up again and everything will be absolutely *amazing*.
>
> Your mates will always be there to catch you when you fail. Or if you fall, actually. So you'll be OK. Nothing to worry about. Right?

He gets a brief flash of Mikey falling off the edge.

> Flailing about like a carrier bag in the wind.
>
> I get knocked down...

He stops, realising who he's talking about, and it hits him.

I always fucking hated that song...

TRANSITION

HANGOVER

A tannoy. Ryan's trainer shop. Shanice has had enough. Ryan's sitting against the back wall. He's shut down.

SHANICE: This is an announcement for Ryan. For the fourth time of asking can you please come to the front tills.

RYAN 1: I've had hangovers before. Like really bad ones. The sort where your hair hurts and you just want to crawl into bed till the world stops spinning.

RYAN 2: But this was worse than that.

RYAN 3: Always got told blokes aren't supposed to cry, are they? You're just brave and do what you can until the feelings go away – at least that's what my Dad's always taught me.

RYAN 1: Strong grown up advice there from Big Nige. Completely fucking pointless.

RYAN 4: You see it on TV or in films and it's usually ridiculous. Ian Beale on EastEnders or footballers crying when they win the World Cup or whatever but it's not like that in real life, is it?

RYAN 1: And I couldn't cry, like not really, not for ages. It was like something had overloaded my system. Couldn't compute anything because someone had pulled all the wires out.

RYAN 2: Spent days after just like some zombie. My brain was properly fucked. Sometimes I'd be fine, just living my life like nothing had happened and then there'd be these other days when I'd just be a complete mess.

RYAN 3: Some days it was just enough to put one foot in front of the other.

RYAN 4: I'd have these weird dreams. Insane nightmares where everything I'd ever said or done wrong would come back and chase me, or I'd be stuck somewhere calling out looking for Mikey and he wouldn't be there.

RYAN 1: Waking up the next morning just wanting to pull the covers over my head and sleep forever.

RYAN 2: Or landing with a bang and waking up in a cold sweat wondering what the fuck was going on.

RYAN 3: Yeah, those days were the worst.

RYAN 4: Never told anyone. Wonder if the others felt the same. Probably should have called someone. Talked to someone.

RYAN 1: But we don't do that either – do we? Talk I mean.

RYAN 2: There was this one day at work, and I'd gone, like lost it. People are asking me about whether we've got Nike Air Maxes in a size 8 or whatever and I'm just standing there looking at them.

RYAN 3: My boss is getting more and more pissed off with me. I can hear her huffing about and throwing boxes around in the stockroom.

RYAN 4: I want to tell her that it's like the world is caving in and I'm so tired that I can't handle it any more but I can't string a sentence together.

RYAN 1: And she's just yelling at me because I've been lacing up this same pair of trainers for about an hour, just staring into space. Like I'm watching everything down this long, dark tunnel.

As Shanice, a different voice.

RYAN 2: *For fuck's sake Ryan can you get off your arse and do something - there's customers out there want serving!*

RYAN 3: And I'm trying. Forcing myself to get through the shift. But in the end she tells me to go home early.

I Don't remember how I got there.

RYAN 4: One foot in front of the other. Whatever it takes.

RYAN 1: I get in through the front door, head straight upstairs and into the bathroom, and just stand under the shower and hope that I feel better.

RYAN 2: It's like I can't do it fast enough. Something's taken over me and I'm just acting on instinct.

RYAN 3: I'd run away if I could but there's nowhere to run to. Besides, soaking wet, so…

Shrugs a bit. Like he knows it's ridiculous.

RYAN 4: I've always started with the water cold and turn it up after a few seconds, I dunno why, just to wake myself up in the morning or whatever.

RYAN 1: But this time I just turn it to the coldest setting and leave it there.

RYAN 2: In my head, I'm telling myself this is insane, like I'm actually aware that I'm possibly going mad and losing my mind somehow.

RYAN 3: But I can't feel anything. It's like all the pain receptors in my brain have stopped working.

The sound of the water running.

RYAN 4: I don't know how long I'm standing there for, like that. Must have been a while.

RYAN 1: In the background there's this bang on the door.

RYAN 2: *Ryan can you get a move on please?*

RYAN 3: My Dad's kicking off because he wants to go for a slash or whatever, and he's getting pissed off because I won't answer him

RYAN 4: *Shit.*

RYAN 2: *Come on – you're taking the piss now. Hurry up will ya?*

RYAN 1: This isn't some territorial Alpha Male fight over the bathroom in the morning. My brain is shutting down.

RYAN 4: I can hear him getting more and more stressed out on the other side of the door and I can't find the words to say anything to tell him what's wrong because it feels like the world is ending.

RYAN 2: *Son, are you alright in there?*

RYAN 1: And as he bangs some more it's like this wall breaks inside me and I start crying. Like properly full on heaving under this freezing cold water.

RYAN 3: I want to be sick, and I can't, and it just sort of engulfs me in wave after wave of this black awfulness.

RYAN 1: It pushes me to the floor, and I just sort of pull myself into this weird foetal position and start to sob. And I can't stop it.

RYAN 2: It's broken me, and it won't stop.

RYAN 4: Like I've fucked it all up, haven't I? I've fucked up my life and his too, and everyone around me.

RYAN 1: And I can just see Mikey's face as it disappears over the edge…

RYAN 2: It's going to feel like this forever. Isn't it? I don't think I can live with it, not anymore.

RYAN 1: Doesn't matter how many times I tell myself it was an accident because *IT'S NEVER GOING TO BE THE SAME.*

RYAN 2: *Right – screw this son, I'm coming in.*

RYAN 1: No Dad, don't, please...

RYAN 4: The door goes, Dad bursts in.

RYAN 1: And all I can hear through the sound of the shower is –

RYAN 2: *Jesus Christ, Ryan –*

RYAN 3: And the water dies away as he turns off the shower.

My useless Dad. Big, red faced Nige. Absolutely unprepared for what awaits him behind the bathroom door.

RYAN 2: *What the bloody hell's the matter?*

Pause. Change of pace.

RYAN 4: You know, I've never known what to make of my old man. We've always sort of lived in this strange world where we occasionally bump into each other on the way to work or whatever, the occasional pint in the pub where we talk about the weather or last night's football or when he thinks he's being clever and texts me a Dad joke when he's trying to be funny.

RYAN 1: Never been one to discuss his feelings, bless him. So fuck knows what he must have made of his only son sitting on the floor of the shower drenched and completely naked, howling to himself because he's fucked up his life.

RYAN 3: I've never been in that situation before. But right then it was like he understood, like he knew what the right thing to do was.

RYAN 4: He pulls out this towel and wraps it round me, and I can barely lift my head off my knees.

RYAN 1: *Dad – you're going to get soaked.*

RYAN 2: *Doesn't matter son. I've seen worse.*

One of them pulls Ryan towards him and gives him a long, protective, parental hug.

RYAN 4: We didn't need any more words. I don't think he ever told my Mum, and they tell each other everything.

RYAN 2: Just me and my Dad.

RYAN 3: And it didn't matter. Because in that moment, and in a point of time that only we would ever know about, I needed someone else to tell me it was going to be OK.

RYAN 1: Because it needed to be OK – more than anything in the world.

TRANSITION

__GANDALF__

DEANO. Fag packet, from somewhere where you wouldn't expect him to be. He's trying to tie a black tie on for a funeral (unsuccessfully...)

He gives up.

DEANO: Well that's fucking pointless isn't it? What do I need a tie for? What am I? Some sort of wanker in a bank!?

He sits for a second. Thinks. Then to a member of the audience who is unlikely to have a light.

    Sorry mate. You got a light? Nah. Didn't think so.

To someone else.

    How about you?

To the tech, who is initially deeply unaware of what's going on.

    Oi Mate. are you sure you don't have one?

TECH: What?

DEANO: Yeah?

The tech is very unimpressed at being picked on.

TECH: Mate, I just work here so –

DEANO: Nah, didn't think so. Not much point after last night and you telling me off for "setting fire to shit." Is there?

>   Yeah, sorry about that, by the way. Good you
>   put the fire out quickly though. I quite like this
>   place. Be a shame if it burnt down.

He thinks a minute. Still to the tech, who replies in unison.

>   *Too soon*, isn't it? Thought so.

Change of subject. With his tie.

>   Hey. Can I leave this with you?

TECH: What's that?

DEANO: It's a tie mate, what else would it be. Here what does this do?

He goes and starts fiddling the lighting desk.

TECH: *Oh come on, don't touch the buttons...*

DEANO: Too Late!

TECH: For Fuck's sake Deano...

DEANO: Hey. Did I ever tell you about that time somebody left a goat in my garden?

TECH: What?

DEANO: No honestly. True story. Come downstairs one day and there's a fucking goat in the garden. Just came down one morning and it's just there, chewing grass like it lived there. Looking at me like I'm supposed to know what to do next. Turns out my brother's mate *Fat Wayne* had decided to "liberate" it from the City Farm while he was high on MDMA one night and now the police were looking for it – so of course the best place he could think to leave it was round at ours because nobody would find it. Stuff like that was always happening in our house. All the fucking time. I dunno why I was surprised.

Fucking ridiculous.

So what do you do?

He shrugs.

OK then.

Well you make the best of it I suppose. Hide it when the guy comes to read the meter. Distract the kid who works Saturdays in Pets at Home and slide a massive pallet of hay into the back of Ryan's SEAT Ibiza. *No questions asked mate. Whatever you want.*

Because I don't mean to get all RSPCA about it but who you going to call? – *GOATBUSTERS?*

Who the fuck do you call and say *"Excuse me, but can you help me, someone's left a fucking GOAT in the back yard?"* Your Mum and Dad? Have to drag them out of Wetherspoons first. Your brother? *"Oh Mate I would but I'm staying round Shelley's at the moment"* – and why's that then? Because he owes some blokes a shitload of money and he can't be in in case they "pop round" and say hello. Turns out that Jason is allergic to animals, *wetwipe*, and the goat absolutely hated Andy so that rules them out doesn't it?

So it's me and my mate. Gandalf. And he must have been there for weeks. And we sort of bonded. You know? Spending our days sitting outside having a fag. Me talking, him listening, just like I am to you now. Trying to solve the world's problems together. And I know it sounds like a weird fucking friendship to have but it worked, you know? I provided for his basic needs, and tried not to piss him off and in return he kept the grass short and didn't ask me to play FIFA with him.

The only other person he took a shine too was Mikey, so I don't know what that says about his taste level but there you go.

To the tech

Are you sure you don't have a light mate?

Tech shakes head, no.

Fuck's sake. Anyway, one day a few weeks later I came home and it was gone. Just like that. Fucked off and nobody knew what happened to it. I doubt Wayne got off his fat arse long enough to take it back to the farm so who knows what happened to it? Empty garden. No more fags in the garden with Gandalf.

Looked everywhere. Called everyone I could think of. Maybe just like everyone else it had

>enough of the chaos and wanted something else from his life. Maybe he'd had enough of the vortex of chaos that was the Dean Family. I mean who knows?

Pause. He's irritated now.

>See that's the thing, isn't it? If I learned anything about life it's that you can't rely on people, can you? People are shit. They let you down. Fuck you up. Tell you that they're going to be there and then never are. The bad ones are too busy either thinking about their own lives or too busy getting battered in the pub to care. Even the good ones disappear in the end. *Can't even look after a fucking goat properly!*

He stops a minute.

>Even your mates disappear eventually.

His anger's given way to sadness now. It's not sure whether he's talking about Mikey or the goat.

>I really liked him. He was sound, he really was…

>It's just that sometimes you want something nice for yourself. You know? A nice day in a park. Your Mum remembers your birthday. People or family who don't fuck off and leave you to fend for yourself and work it out forever on your own. Someone to just sit and listen without trying to fix it or say something really fucking stupid when your mate dies in a horrible

> accident which you couldn't help, even though you really want to. One day I'd like to not have to walk this earth on my own. Be nice, wouldn't it?

He ponders for a minute. Thinking.

> Still think about him sometimes. *Gandalf I mean.* Sitting in the garden, eating grass. Whether it had a nice life, whether it's happy somewhere. Hoping that it never ended up in a curry. You know. Simple things.

Philosophical pause.

> Guess the thing about looking after yourself is that you can't be disappointed when it all turns to shit around you. Can you?

He turns to go. As he does the tech calls him back.

TECH: *Hey Deano. You forgot something.*

The tech hands Deano back his tie, but it's been done up for him properly, like a parent would. Like a gift.

DEANO: Oh mate. Seriously?

TECH: You'll be alright. I promise.

Deano smiles. Chuffed. Back to his old self.

DEANO: Ah thanks mate. You're alright you are. I'll even go and smoke this outside though. See you in a bit. Yeah? (*And he's off...*)

TRANSITION

__FIX YOU__

The four of them form a funeral procession. Standing over Mikey's coffin.

RYAN 1: Funerals don't feel like they're for the person that died, do they? They're really only for the people you leave behind.

RYAN 2: Big black cars pulling up at some church somewhere. People standing in huddled corners whispering quietly to themselves.

RYAN 3: Doing their best to keep their shit together.

RYAN 4: Nothing about Mikey's funeral felt like his actual life. It was weird and I hated everything about it.

RYAN 1: There must have been 150 people there. Everyone crammed into this little church. His massive family, Mum and Dad and all those brothers and sisters, all dressed in black, like the mafia had come to town.

RYAN 2: And there's all our families too. Our Mums and Dads and everyone we went to school with. My Mum's squashed Big Nige into a suit and told him to behave himself. Doesn't feel right – They're all standing a respectful distance away. most of them probably grateful that it's not their kid they're burying.

The biggest news in that town all year.

RYAN 1: My Mum goes over and gives Andy's Mum a hug. I guess you forget that they all know each other too.

RYAN 3: How come you know what to do at a funeral even though nobody ever sits you down and tells you what you're supposed to do?

RYAN 4: Doesn't feel right. The people that are here all feel out of place. Like someone's died in the wrong order.

RYAN 1: But that's because he shouldn't be dead. Should he?

They go to pick up the coffin.

RYAN 2: We're carrying the coffin. Course we are. The universe is shit like that. The four of us hanging on to him and each other for dear life.

RYAN 3: You never think that you're going to have to carry your mate's body into some church, Do you? Watch his Mum and Dad crying – Leanne staring at us with utter hate as we pass because in her eyes we should have done something to stop it.

Out of the corner of their mouths, like they're whispering.

RYAN 1: We're walking, slowly, linking arms under the weight of that wood, and all I can think about is how his life's over now and this is all so wrong.

RYAN 2: Eyes on the end. try not to fall over. Try not to get upset. Try not to fuck it up.

RYAN 3: As we're walking all I can think of are the things he's never going to get to do now.

RYAN 4: Stag dos, lads trips away, cheering at the FA Cup final in some grotty pub somewhere.

RYAN 1: Kebabs at closing time and singing crap songs in the street battered at 2am. Five-A-Side football games and family holidays to Spain.

RYAN 2: 6am pints in a Wetherspoons at the airport.

RYAN 3: Jumping around to the Kaiser Chiefs at midnight in that same hotel in town where all of us get married one after the other in shiny suits that we're only going to wear once.

RYAN 4: He was going to be a Dad, you know? Now that little girl of his is gonna grow up without ever knowing who he was.

RYAN 1: Taking his kids to McDonald's at the weekends and letting them ride on his back in the garden.

RYAN 2: Telling his daughter when she grows up that she'll always be his princess and terrifying the fuck out of her boyfriends for the rest of his life, because nobody will ever be good enough.

RYAN 3: Taking his grandkids for walks on Sunday afternoons with a pocket full of polo mints and a stick for the dog.

RYAN 4: Getting old together with the rest of us. Swapping football shirts and Calvin Kleins for jumpers from M&S in five different shades of brown and falling asleep in front of the telly on Christmas Day.

RYAN 1: Moaning about our dodgy knees which used to have the perfect left foot (except you, Jase…)

RYAN 2: Forgetting it all as everything he ever remembers slips away a bit at a time.

RYAN 3: Because that's how he should have lived his life, right? Isn't it? Closing his eyes at some ripe old age in some warm bed, charming the nurses to death surrounded by everyone he ever loved.

RYAN 4: Not having his mates carry him away and lower him into a hole for people to throw earth at.

RYAN 1: He's never gonna have any of that now, is he?

He catches himself.

Breaks a minute.

They look at each other.

RYAN 3: Oh and did I mention that they played *Fix You by Coldplay* as we took the coffin down the aisle?

Yeah fuck that.

RYAN 2: If I'd had chance, I'd step in. Do something about it. Try and stop it before it was too late. Do whatever we could to stop it all from happening.

RYAN 4: He's like this broken clock, you know? Stopped at a point in time. He deserved all those things, and so much more. He deserved to get old.

RYAN 1: And it's not fucking fair. Is it?

It's just not fair…

TRANSITION

DRY YOUR EYES, MATE

The four of them at Mikey's wake, later in the day. Bleary, heavy, sad.

RYAN 1: So you know I said Mikey came from this massive family? Well I wasn't joking. Turns out they hired some Irish working men's club in town and threw him this ridiculous wake.

RYAN 4: Do you throw a wake? Is that a thing?

RYAN 2: Yeah well, I dunno what that was but it was excruciating.

RYAN 3: Turns out his family's way of coping was to sling a shit load of beige Iceland food at the problem and wash it down with gallons of Guinness till you can barely see any more...

RYAN 2: ...because that was the best way of dealing with it, apparently.

RYAN 1: Crammed into this boiling room with 1970's wallpaper and a photo of him at the end taken on his 21st birthday. Talking.

RYAN 2: Trying to be polite and avoid the elephant in the room.

RYAN 4: And it was a fucking *Tuesday* as well. Proper grim. Who wants to get wasted on Guinness on a Tuesday afternoon.

Nah.

He takes a hip flask out of his pocket and drinks from it.

RYAN 3: (*interrupts*) There's this one point, towards the end, I look round the room and I'm sort of on my own – dunno where everyone else is, they've all sort of drifted away.

RYAN 4: I realise that I'm so done with it. The booze and the fake smiling and the trying to be brave. Talking to his Aunties who keep saying what a shame it is and trying to avoid Leanne's eye because she blames us for what happened.

RYAN 1: Then in the corner of the room I can hear someone singing.

The first lines of "The Fields of Athenry"

MIKEY'S DAD: *By a lonely prison wall... I heard a young girl calling...*

RYAN 2: It's Mikey's Dad. He's sort of on the corner of the dancefloor of this place, not that anyone's dancing. On his own, blind drunk.

MIKEY'S DAD: *"Michael, they have taken you away..."*

RYAN 3: He's singing. Swaying. Red eyes, tie undone, lurching around the room singing this song to himself - like he doesn't give a shit who can hear him.

RYAN 4: Nobody stops him, nobody tells him to be quiet. We're all just watching him crying for the son he lost.

RYAN 3: I think it's the saddest thing I've ever seen.

Breaks off.

RYAN 2: Nah, can't handle it. It's too hot and too awkward, and that song makes no fucking sense – so I try and find somewhere with some fresh air instead.

RYAN 1: I look out and two floors down I can see these three figures downstairs just standing in the car park outside, and I know that that's exactly where I need to be.

TRANSITION

BEER BOTTLE

The four of them standing in the car park outside. Each holding a bottle of beer, Deano with his hip flask.

RYAN 1: Turns out they'd all had the same idea. Course they did.

RYAN 2: The four of us standing there in this car park, just looking at each other.

RYAN 3: All of us more or less dressed the same, except for Deano who's got a ridiculous pair of sunglasses on. Just leaning against this wall in clouds of smoke.

RYAN 4: And even then, there's a hole missing where our mate should be, and it hurts, but of course, nobody's going to draw attention to it first.

RYAN 1: Fuck me, it's a bit much in there.

RYAN 3: You alright mate?

RYAN 2: And I'm not sure. I just keep thinking that none of this feels right. But it doesn't seem right to say anything, so I don't.

RYAN 1: *Yeah, I'm alright, yeah. Just needed to get the fuck out of there. You know?*

RYAN 3: Was he still singing?

RYAN 1: Who, Mikey's Dad? Yeah he was. It was a bit grim if I'm honest.

RYAN 2: Not much chance of him winning The Voice any time soon, is there?

Awkward Silence.

RYAN 3: So, I have a question. Why is it that every Irish event that you ever go to they always sing that stupid song? Doesn't matter if it's a wedding or a funeral or just because it's some random Tuesday. Stick a load of Irish people in a room, get everyone battered and someone will always sing "The Fields of Athenry?"

They sort of look at him. Where's that come from? Ryan snaps at him –

RYAN 1: *I dunno mate – because maybe if we all sang along to Westlife instead it would be a bit inappropriate – Do you know what I mean?*

RYAN 3: Yeah I suppose.

RYAN 1: Just leave it. Yeah?

RYAN 3: Sorry. Was just saying…?

Awkward silence. After a few seconds.

RYAN 2: This is weird, right?

RYAN 3: What do you mean?

RYAN 1: The funeral, this whole day. Being here. doesn't feel right.

RYAN 3: You're not wrong there, mate.

RYAN 1: Like, it's just weird we're going to have to get used to him not being here anymore?

RYAN 2: Everyone's kind of looking at their feet. Nobody wants to say anything.

RYAN 3: I notice Deano shifting against the wall and he just sort of looks at me.

RYAN 4: Yeah it's weird and yeah it's sad, but this is normal life isn't it? We're all told all the time that this is all there is, like everything round here stays the same. We're supposed to believe that he was gonna grow old forever but maybe this was exactly how things were supposed to turn out?

RYAN 1: What do you mean by that Deano? Don't be a prick.

RYAN 4: No, right, listen. What I mean is, that maybe this was the way his life was always supposed to be? Like his destiny was always to be just what happened. Maybe he wasn't supposed to spend his life waiting for the weekend to get shitfaced. Falling over. Popping out a hundred kids with Leanne just like his Dad did. And I don't want to get all Elton John about it but it's *the circle of fucking life mate*. I'm telling you. Do you know what I mean?

Andy snaps back now. Snippy.

RYAN 3: Does that make you feel better? Because to me that sounds like shite.

RYAN 4: Yeah, it does actually, because I choose to believe that this isn't all mapped out for us. Life doesn't have to be determined by the fact that we're all supposed to live and die in this shithole, no matter what the universe or your family or my family or his family might have to say about it.

He's kinda right, even if it's weird.

That being said though, I saw the priest trip over at the graveside and I know for a fact that Mikey's drunk Aunty Kathleen gave Jason her phone number and told him to call her.

So you know, life goes on, doesn't it Jase?

RYAN 2: Oh fuck off, Deano.

RYAN 3: Which one is Aunty Kathleen? Not the old one with the teeth and the hair...?

RYAN 4: No, gross. The one at the bar with the fags. Leopard Print. The proper Kat Slater one. She said something about needing her guttering doing one day, so...

RYAN 1: Yeah mate, that's exactly what his horny divorced aunty wanted.

Properly in there, you are, Jason.

The penny drops...

RYAN 2: *Fuck's sake, Ryan.*

And they all look at each other. Winding him up. Laughter.

RYAN 1: Fuck me, that's hilarious. First time I've laughed in ages.

RYAN 4: Can't score on the pitch Jase but you can score at a funeral. Well proud of you mate!

RYAN 2: Fuck off Deano!

RYAN 1: I was thinking – today, this funeral, or whatever it is, it doesn't feel like we got chance to say goodbye to him properly, like in a way he would have wanted.

RYAN 4: We literally carried him to a hole in the ground and buried him mate, what are you talking about?

RYAN 1: Nah I'm not saying that. Coldplay, his Dad crying, whatever. It's all bullshit. We can do better than that, can't we?

Listen, what I'm saying, that we should try and let go, Tell him what we think. Do it properly.

They look at each other. A big decision to be made. He looks around for reassurance.

RYAN 3: Yeah, I think you're right.

And Deano puts down his fag, steps forward. Looks at the others.

Pause.

RYAN 4: Alright then. I'll go first, dickheads. This is weird, innit?

>Ohh Mikey, fuck me, you were alright, you were. I mean you were sometimes a bit flakey and I'm always going to be completely terrified of your Mum, but you were always sound to me. *Nice one. Cheers.*

And he holds his bottle up in a toast.

Jason up next. Challenge Accepted.

RYAN 2: I remember, Year 9, first time I broke up with a girl – my heart was proper broken. He was brilliant, he was. Gave me this plastic fish with "Plenty more in the sea" written on it in permanent marker. Still got it in my bedroom. He told me that it would be OK and you know what, it was, in the end. *I miss you mate.*

Bottle up. Andy next.

RYAN 3: I used to look at you sometimes and you used to blow my mind a bit. Always smiling. Saw the best in us, I think. Didn't matter if it was that day we all got wasted on the strip in Faliraki or outside that bloody kebab shop at 3 in the morning. He always found something to laugh about. Guess I'll finally get that Foo Fighters album back too now as well. So yeah. *Thanks for making me laugh too.*

Bottle up. They look at Ryan.

RYAN 1: Alright. Looks like I'm last to go then.

> I don't know if you can hear me but I hope wherever you are you're having the best time. I hope that there'll always be a pint in front of you. I'll try to make sure your little girl knows what a brilliant bloke her dad was, because you deserve it.
>
> And we'll try and do our best. Even if you're not here anymore.

He steps forward. The final bottle in the circle of four. They look at each other.

RYAN 2: Does that work?

RYAN 4: Fine with me.

RYAN 3: Yeah me too.

Collectively, bottles raised.

RYAN 1: To Mikey.

Sort of together, in their own way.

RYAN 2,3,4: *Mikey.*

They clink the bottles together. Cheers. An agreement between them.

TRANSITION

FEEL THE LOVE

Like the beginning, four men have replaced the boys on the back wall fading in over the closing sequence of the show. One of them is noticeably absent.

RYAN 1: Those five boys. Fuck me, what a team. Took a while, but we're alright. And it'll never be the same but we're getting there. Just took some time for us to get over it.

RYAN 2: We're all changing, but that's good, isn't it? We're growing up. I sometimes wonder if we're going to be the first generation to make it out of here and do something different with our lives.

RYAN 3: But there wasn't a lot wrong with it in the first place. Was there?

RYAN 4: Jason finally found himself a girlfriend, one who he wants to stay with for longer than 5 minutes and who actually wants to be in a relationship with him too. They're getting married next Summer.

Manages the under 10's junior football league even though he still can't kick with his left foot for shit!

That stag do is going to be proper carnage.

RYAN 1: Andy's got himself a little shop selling vinyl in town. Properly full of hipster twats. He still walks round with his headphones on like a bell-end. One day we might go on a night out somewhere where he actually likes the music and doesn't try to hijack the DJ when he's drunk.

RYAN 2: Deano's still a legend. Turns out he saved all that money from all those schemes of his and had been putting the cash into a savings account like a proper adult. Bought his first flat in town. Can you fucking believe it?

RYAN 3: Yeah but we still found him absolutely battered at 6 in the morning last Sunday wearing just a sombrero in a shopping trolley singing to himself. Turns out you can teach an old dog new tricks.

RYAN 4: Leanne had her little girl. She's got a new bloke now but Mikey'll always be that kid's Dad.

I see them round town sometimes and try not to think about that list of all the things they would have done together.

I hope they're both happy.

RYAN 1: Life went back to normal for me, in the end. Sacked off the trainer shop though and got a job in an office instead. Pays the bills. My Mum still gets pissed off about having to pick up my boxers off the floor and my Dad still sends me crap jokes on WhatsApp.

Confesses.

We never talk about that day I lost it in the shower.

RYAN 4: I wonder if that experience. The balcony, the fall, that flashbang going off that night was the one thing that changed everything for all of us forever.

And maybe that's what Mikey meant to all of us.

Summing up. Bringing it together.

RYAN 3: You know, I said at the start I'd never had a brother, but I don't think that's right. Those boys in that photo were the closest thing I'd ever get.

My best mates…

RYAN 2: And our "squad" or whatever we're allowed to call it may get bigger, or some of the personnel might change. Maybe over the years we'll add wives and girlfriends and kids of our own to the mix, but we'll always have each other.

RYAN 4: Maybe we'll be like our parents in 20 year's time. Doing the same stuff over and over, and our kids will look back at what we wore and the music we listened to in horror because it's all so fucking shameful mate.

RYAN 3: But we'll tell them stories, the ones about growing up in this random little town where nothing ever happens, because let's face it, nobody's going to do it for us, are they? And maybe those kids won't be too embarrassed when we tell them how we used to go out and

>   get smashed in nightclubs dancing to Calvin
>   Harris or about that day we all got sunstroke in
>   Kavos.

He smiles, knowingly.

RYAN 2:   Because no matter how big the "gang" gets, we'll
                 always be the same.

                 We'll always be the coolest.

RYAN 1:   So tonight, we're doing it properly. Fuck that
                 funeral and all those people standing around
                 talking in a car park in the cold. That wasn't
                 him. That's not us – is it? We're going to go out,
                 drink far more than we should, dance ourselves
                 stupid to ridiculous music and celebrate his life.
                 Make the best of everything we have because
                 who knows how long we've all got.

                 There's a pause. Bringing it all together. No
                 matter what happens, we'll always be those five
                 little boys in that photograph.

To the audience, honest now.

>   I can't go back in time and tell them that they'll
>   make it – that they'll grow up to be anything
>   other than what the universe had planned for
>   them in advance. That they'll do anything more
>   than live and die in this little town.
>
>   But there's nothing wrong with that. Is there?
>
>   We'll always have each other.

He smiles.

> My brothers – and nobody will ever take that away from us, not ever.

The four of them are on stage now, together. Brothers together standing in a real-life replica of the photo behind them. Jason turns and puts his hand on Ryan's shoulder.

RYAN 2: Are you alright, mate?

RYAN 1: Nah mate. I don't think I am. But it's OK. I will be.

> One day…

And the lights go down and "Feel the Love" by Rudimental plays as they start the best night out ever (and the rest of their lives.)

CURTAIN